Roses

TREVI BENNETT

ROSES

Inquiries for reprint permission to: PO Box 1335
Aspen CO 81612 or kayarebel@me.com

The names of individuals in this book have been
changed to protect their identities.

Summary: Terra's journal and dream journal
entries discussing life, death and change.
Understanding labels and old recordings is the key
to finding her peace. She and Jona choose to focus
on solutions, positive manifestations, psychic
connections and love.

Roses by Trevi Bennett – Volume 1

ISBN-13: 978-0615579399 (Kayarebel)

First printing 2012
The text for this book is set in Verdana

[Body, Mind & Spirit / Inspiration & Personal
Growth]

LOVINGLY DEDICATED

to Steve Sanders and David Sanders

ACKNOWLEDGMENTS

Infinite thanks to my mom and dad for your warmth, compassion and enduring love. I am eternally grateful for every sacrifice you have made on behalf of your uncensored daughter.

Respect and unending love to my incredible husband for believing in my *dreams* and aspirations, weetie power!

I wish to empower free expression and the sharing of alternative knowledge. It is an extraordinary time in space and the energy put forth by everyone will allow an elevated focus on love and acceptance to arise.

TABLE OF CONTENTS

ROSES

Part One

1 | Evolving extinction

Wavy brown hair to my shoulders, pale skin and brown eyes are my defining attributes. I'm currently growing my hair out which is connecting me with the earth and universal grid, I can feel it. Engaged and soon to be married, Jona and I are beginning a new year, it feels like a *dream*. Playful yet calm he is my balance and music is his balance.
With a gentle nature that manifests itself in honest wisdom he often says, "Whatever the problem, we can always work it out."

Jona's cousin Desmond is also a music lover and thrives on the excitement of the scene. Darkly dyed hair that was undoubtedly blond in his youth is now slicked and spiked dependent upon his mood. A bit of makeup or nail polish is not unheard of, unless you ask someone in denial of his flamboyant side.

2 | Energy flash
Rolling runner

1.2   It's a New Year again and we tried to go out, but it was so expensive we came home by 11:00pm. Kind of disappointing, but I was glad I was with Jona. He's supportive and cool, plus we laugh and have fun together. Honestly I've had a rough time since we've gotten engaged and the stress has not eased yet. All I can think about is the flowers, cake, rings, bridesmaid and flower girl dresses, invitations, favors, and my dress fitting, whew!

I was feeling overwhelmed yesterday and my friend suggested I go on medication. Wow! Nothing straightens me out more than thinking of the cruel medicinal alternative. I felt better almost immediately. If it were up to the doctors I'd be drugged out and would never act up again, 1,000mg Depakote;

600mg Seroquel; 900mg Lithium. If I had continued my medication they prescribed I'd literally have Ataxic Dysarthia and not be able to function. Plus the $1,000 monthly bill is always fun.

The ironic twist to asking for help is the permanent condition the doctors could give you. Inadvertently I signed up for the label of depression, and now manic depression. Seriously think, are you truly off? Do you feel things are wrong?

Maybe you are spoiled, bored, or simply conditioned to perpetuate your own discontent. Whatever the instance I don't believe drugs have ever helped me, at least not the ones prescribed for my evasive brain chemistry.

The catch 22 of having a mental illness is, you are sick if you take medication and sick if you don't. If you chose a path other than medication it confirms you are sick. However, medication does not guarantee that you won't act up. In all probability you will experience a backlash from trusting wholeheartedly in an exterior solution instead of looking within.

1/3   Love heals all wounds. A soft heart and a hard head do not mix, yet they both can have moments in time.

1/30   Last night Jona played at Syzgy, it went off! He also played at the Funky Buddha recently, I loved his set. Jona's brother and cousin Desmond even came out with a few friends.

Next day we tasted cake, it's going to be white/ivory with peach/pink roses, also various shaped layers; octagon, square and round. One layer will be pound cake, the other layers will be chocolate chip with ganache and vanilla filling. I finally found my bridesmaid dresses in town---Ingwa Malero Virgo dress in Pearl, lace halter top with cream chiffon empire waist. Five months to go!

Today an old interest called from Jamaica, he congratulated me and said, "Maybe next time I see you I'll meet your husband and baby."

Out of the blue last week another old interest called and said, "I'm in town." (Drop everything, Mr. Ego has arrived.)

I told him, "I'm on my way to Denver with my fiancé who's playing a gig."

Whoa, he was blown away, shocked is more the term. The next day yet another old interest called, my past was catching up to me it seems. He and his friend were in town for the X-Games. The following day they met Jona and we all hung at the house. I saw a picture of his 2 year old son, I guess the wife is in Costa and he's here until spring. I'm glad that's not me, some chick he can ditch and go find other girls?

Totally stoked with Jona, he's the absolute best and I'm glad where I am. The drama seems mundane to write about, I'm over trying to maintain high maintenance friendships.

I'm getting my art ready to put in a show February 21st, three weeks away. I need to take my last three paintings in for framing.

3 | Bird dog of old

Friend

May 20   It's 4:00am and I can't sleep. I had a headache earlier and laid down before sunset, now I'm fully up. I haven't been taking my activated B^6 and 5-HTP at night, which helps me sleep. I just picked up more from my holistic Doctor today, I will start again tomorrow. I've been taking my fish oil for the last couple days, but need to increase the dosage. Exercising more would probably help me sleep too. I'm really tired lately with a low level of constant anxiety. It must be about the wedding. It's a month from tomorrow and I'm really excited!

A wedding shower is very odd. It feels strange getting gifts for no reason, although you know there's a reason. We've received many considerate gifts from everyone.

The birds have been singing outside my window. There is one bird that has come for the last couple of weeks to the limb outside the small bedroom. It's a Robin that slams against the window repeatedly. Maybe it thinks it's mating?

It's quite disturbing and makes me want to ask the bird, "Why are you hurting yourself?"

That's a good question, I feel the same way. I know smoking sometimes hurts, but I do it because it helps in other ways. I'm definitely thankful to have an alternative perspective, which smoking inevitably gives me. I have come to an unspoken agreement with myself. (Unwritten as well.)

Like most people I love to have a feeling of security in all aspects of my life. The struggle with habituation is human, be it coffee, exercise, work, or chocolate. Blessed to have the love I do in my life, I still believe what is mine will come to me.

I dreamt the other night that I was late to the wedding. As the anxiety mounts---still a few things to do, fill the little bags, stuff the cards with our note, sew the six pence on my shoe, wrap the gifts, write my vows, come up with music and find something special for Jona.

I decided to do a cake pull where all the bridesmaids pull a charm out of the cake, it's an old Victorian tradition. I have sterling silver lotus flower pendants to tie on ribbons and today I found three keys that say dream, peace, and love, which I will tie on the other ends. Then each bridesmaid can choose which key to pull.

Unexplainable, the love we share, grown from many nights up late philosophizing until we created circles of logic beyond our own expectations. Found to be resistant, we both face great challenges of acceptance and release. Release from the pain we thought we had to endure alone. Now free in a new universe of swirling light energies, yet still held back from the ultimate finale. This time expanse will be a life full of abundance and understanding. A world unlimited and bright with possibilities, only accessible together, our eyes sharing the same sights. We are one, born in the same spot and reunited after lifetimes, I am you.

4 | Think of us often

Dazily dreamer

It was absolutely the most gorgeous wedding ever!

One of our friends said, "I've been to weddings since I was 4 years old and yours was the most beautiful."

Jona's Grandma said, "In all my years of going to weddings I've never shed a tear, except at this one. It was the most beautiful wedding I've ever seen, and I've been to my share of weddings!"

June 23rd – July 7th we went to Mexico, it was outstanding!

July 9   I was packing, trying to get all of my things together. I felt pressure to get out of there. House on a cliff, lots of strange bugs. Scared I tried to run but there was a guy I knew that I had to talk to, I was hiding in a room with windows.

7.14   Saturday: Now that I'm married I changed my name with the Social Security office and got a new drivers license too. It's official, my maiden name is gone after 34 years and 20 days.

5 | Close to the heart

Guardian

8.10   Jona and I saw a huge owl fly across the road, in slow motion it seemed, as we were driving by Buttermilk Mountain.

Jona said, "It has a mouse in its claws."

8.22   It is not easy to define, when life is difficult I often look for a solution, a change. What could I do differently, so I would feel ok? The formula is simple, eat when you're hungry, sleep when you're tired, do things that help. Once I feel the results of my efforts I forget how hard it was before. Selective amnesia of sorts. Currently I have not eaten, I've cried numerous times and my sleep is erratic at best. What of that fabulous formula? Can I not follow simplicity? To get off of the illusory track I will just sit with my content, or discontent, as it may be. My old recordings of self, put downs ingrained in a repetitious mind. Misunderstandings, frustration, anger, outbursts, acceptance, rinse, repeat. Misunderstandings, frustration, anger, outbursts, acceptance, rinse, repeat.

Even now the words form slowly. I tell myself everything is fine. I'm fortunate and there is no reason to be sad. Things are great, I have everything I need. Then why the gloomy face? Just natural I guess. The next moment I smile and giggle at a ridiculous headline, or realize something ironic that I've done, my stomach growls. Although the tears were welling in my eyes a moment ago, now I think I'll go eat.

8.23   Maybe I took it as a challenge, but one April day ten years ago someone told me I was disabled, those words ring in my head to this day. Now that I think of it they handed me a piece of paper stating how I was disabled, encouraging me to sign. As if I would verify its legitimacy? I remember ripping it up, somehow proving myself wrong. Reacting is my greatest downfall. Why couldn't I just be? Intent on doing, doing, doing. The point of action was where I wanted to be at all times. Getting something accomplished, taught to be driven, but who's driving is the question.

8.24   Cause and effect, that's all it is. The choices I've made in my life have led me to where I am now. I'm married, the absolute last place I ever thought I'd be.

8.29   Last night I heard a noise that sounded like a goose. After ten minutes I finally went to the window to see what it was. A tiny black bear cub seemed to be lost from his mom and was yelping, more like bleating, to find her again. It was adorable. All I wanted to do was help, but I know better than to get in between a baby bear and its mama. If only

I could be so wise every time I wanted to help.

I got sick last week with a head cold and it's impossible to breathe. Every time I lay down in bed I end up in a coughing fit. I've spent weeks sleeping fitfully on the couch and I miss Jona. I ordered a new silk mattress cover to help regulate the heat that the foam mattress gives off and an allergy cover too. I should be sleeping better in the next few weeks. Until then I'll be a tired, grumpy one.

8.30   I'm positive that Jona's father will recover soon. He was diagnosed with colon cancer and had surgery yesterday. I guess everything looks good, except maybe his lymph glands. It's hard since he also has MS and took all these experimental drugs to cure it. Who knows what those drugs did?

6 | Alarming bark

Constantly curious

9/3   Jona was there, house with cobblestone driveway by the ocean.

9.3   Today is Labor Day so I got to chill at home. Jona treats me really well. He gives me food money so I eat lunch. I never would've imagined being his wife would be this different.

I said, "I need more therapy," and he whips out a $100 for me to go get a massage.

I'm stoked we're married. I love him, he's all my dreams come true.

9.4   I spoke with Jona a few times today. He's visiting his Dad in the hospital. It's incredibly difficult to heal in a hospital, surrounded by prodding, worried people, drugs and televisions in every room.

Today the most amazing news is that our wedding announcement came out in The Aspen Times Weekly. It just happens to be the 1st Best of Aspen issue, how perfect. What awesome timing.

9/9   It was dark and I was walking on a path. Everything was getting fuzzy, blurry. I woke up and thought to myself I should find Jona quick. I was moving so slow I could barely make it to the bedroom door. I turned the knob and was screaming, "Jona," but only whispers would come out. I remember shaking him, screaming his name, trying to wake him up.

9/12   My friend told me my foam knock-off bed is toxic. I can't believe it, oh yes, I guess

I can. Every time I lay down in that bed I can't breathe. I'm stoked to finally know I'm not too picky, I'm actually allergic. It's going to change, whatever the shift may be it will be welcome.

9/13   Something happened where the world had changed. I was with Jona on a bus full of people. We were looking out the windows at all the changes. Then we were alone on the bus determining how to defend ourselves next time.

9/15   I saw my cranial sacral therapist the other day and I feel much more balanced. I guess talking to him allows me to be in the present just by remembering what I already know. Although this existence is an illusion that we project, it is also very real. You are what you want and you want what you are. I can never be in just one moment and I never know what may happen in the next moment. Like it or not you too do not know what may happen in the next moment. Creating a mass complication out of simplicity is what the mind does best. I can argue with just being all day, or I can accept that we all simply exist. The definitions in my mind that justify right and wrong have all been learned. Primates are social animals that mimic.

9/21   Last night I opened for King Yellowman. It was awesome I played an hour set on the CD-J's vinyl setting of course. I felt right at home. The mixer was sick too.

Jona said, "It was the best one yet!"

It sounded great, can't wait to play again. Yellowman was incredible energy, high stepping roots. After missing him in Italy I'm glad I finally got to see him, even open for him, nonetheless.

Midnite is coming next week, October 2nd.
That guy from the band called me last night.
It's odd hearing from him after all that
happened in Hawaii. Maybe he blocked it out
too? Either way I will be strong. Jona got me
six white roses yesterday, he is sweet.

9/22   My head feels like it's going to
explode. All the anger at things I can't explain.
Why do people have to suffer? Because that's
life? I find that to be a sh*tty excuse. We
suffer because we chose to suffer, inevitably?
I say that I can't help feeling bad, but all the
while it is I who propels the negative message
in my mind, repetitious mind. I know that
smoking marijuana helps immensely.

I feel calm and normal after I take a toke.
Usually I have to drive myself to the end of
the line before I remember to do something
that helps. I'll even stare at it indefinitely and
not smoke, just knowing it is there.
Immediately I have my senses back. I can

logically think about my next move instead of being afflicted by emotion. Everything is relative again. Nothing is worth ending it over a little emotion. I'm glad that there is a natural, healing herb such as marijuana.

It settles my nerves and serves as an appetite stimulant. It helps me sleep and generally soothes any physical ailments I may experience day to day. Be it a headache, stomachache, backache, or heartbreak marijuana helps every time. I know marijuana has saved my life countless times. The only time anyone died from marijuana was when a ½ ton brick was accidentally dropped in transport and crushed a man. It's true!

- Taxpayers spend roughly $7.7 billion on marijuana prohibition annually.
- 100,000 people die of alcohol use annually.
- 440,000 people die of tobacco use annually.

· Even acetaminophen killed 458 people last year.

Marijuana caused ZERO deaths, why the huge drug war? Propaganda still seeps from the governmental pores, don't be fooled. I love the commercial where the dog tells his owner he misses her because she's always high. If you're hearing your dog speak English you must be smoking something other than pot. Also, the commercial where the cartoon stick figures are hanging out and the guy starts to smoke. The girl stick figure then leaves the guy for an alien. Seriously, they fly off in his spaceship. What kind of message is that? It seems like the alien and girl took off on something a little heavier than ditch weed.

7 | Finally freedom

Love

10/18   I have calm and balance. I am able to breathe freely. I am successful in life and have the energy of thought. With that energy comes power, the power to alter structures. I love my parents and am glad they are a part of my life. I feel such an intense connection with everything in the world. I am affected by the well being of the whole. Like every living cell in my body, working together is critical to the survival of the whole.

Finding peace with the vibration of this place, even the place within this place, for infinity. The impact of words and sound is undeniable. I've known for a long time that what I think manifests. When I focus on what I know to be beneficial to myself, benefit can only flow outward to others.

All my positive manifestations of becoming a DJ, singer, belly dancer, painter and writer have come true. Even finding true love has manifested.

I remember explaining to my mom the difference in our mind sets. She was convinced I would have another manic episode and wanted to know my plan to avoid this inevitability. I told her my thought was that I am well and whole, that I would not become manic again. Her thought path was reinforcing a future that had not been decided yet. I wanted to reinforce a future of endless possibilities, not limited disappointments. Yes, it's true, I could potentially become manic. Dwelling on this possibility will undoubtedly depress me, hence confirming my label of bi-polar. I have to be well now. I have to be present now. I am responsible for my decisions and I do have choices.

The crutch of a label is not for me. I do not accept this disease, it is something reinforced by the doctors. They say if I don't accept it I am in denial. I say if I accept it I am not in denial. I accept that they think I am sick. However, I know I am well. Their path for me, versus my path for me.

Don't ever let anyone tell you not to trust yourself, that your instincts are wrong. How would someone else possibly know how you feel? Assuming the negative, reinforcing it and giving it a story to remember. Don't forget you're sick, you'll always be sick and you'll never be able to escape this disease. Bullsh*t!

Uneasiness is in the mind, realize that MIND is a concept and suddenly there is nothing to support the thought of uneasiness. You are perfect exactly how you are, no striving to make more money, acquire more things, be skinnier, stronger, or more well liked. You are already loved and supported. You have the strength, will and utter determination to know your thoughts have beneficial power.

Maybe it is too much to think this could be true. That would mean you would have to own what you have done in this world. The weight of how you have potentially affected others is massive. Thankfully though, we don't have to dwell in the past, we can choose to be present.

The illusion that I have to plan things out, or that I have to feel a certain way about past events is false. I can be. That is all I have ever been and ever will be. Now has passed and I've forgotten what was said. The imprint of the experience is still with me though, ingrained in my knowing.

Re-patterning ourselves is already happening. We see the things that bring suffering and instead of resolving to not suffer, we suffer. If war brings pain, don't war. If your environment makes you sick, change your environment. If objectives are more important than human lives, change your objective. There is no question without an alternate answer. Responsibility is in my hands if I decide not to indulge in "their drugs" I better have a well laid plan explaining the alternative.

10.2   Today I went shopping for organic and stocked up. I recently removed everything from our kitchen with partially hydrogenated or hydrogenated oils. I also removed anything with preservatives or artificial flavors like vanillin. I even got rid of our bread with corn syrup as a first ingredient and replaced it with real bread. It snowed 3-4" today for the first time this winter season. Jona's making an incredible tortilla soup and life is sweet. I just went to see the new puppy. Kaya will get along with her just fine, as soon as those puppy sharp teeth are gone.

10/26   Sometimes when I let things flow and don't attach to the past or future something comes out that is amazing. Being present I have many realizations, wondering who my spirit guide is for the first time. I've always felt a presence around me, guiding me towards experience. I remember thirteen years ago I had taken some hallucinogenic mushroom tea. Usually advisable to not look in the mirror when tripping (you could freak out when your face changes), but for some reason I was instantly drawn there.

I had no fear only curiosity, a dangerous combination. As I looked deep in my pupils the blur around my focus took on many forms. An ancient yogi, a regal face of royalty, all the while I held my gaze on my eyes, not even blinking. Then through my felt-sense there were three figures on the other side of the mirror. I like to refer to them as me, myself and I. Although they were a part of me, they also each distinctively held their own energy. One was mischievous, one had calm wisdom, and one was an innocent. Dependent upon the circumstance one or all could make themselves known.

Another time I felt the presence of the three was in San Francisco. It was the first time I was hospitalized for mania. In a dream I had they were above my head on the other side of the wall, looking down on me sleeping. To feel the presence of something divine, to allow it to be without judgment, is just love. Near death experiences solidify the importance of being present now. There is no yesterday or tomorrow, only now. Sometimes the fear wells up inside, I realize I've been hurt and think back to specific turning points my consciousness created something new. It's true, few people understand me when I'm channeling. It's even more true that if I were to be in the correct environment many people would understand. We share life. There is nothing foreign about tuning in with someone that's on your same frequency. There is no point in asking why. We each already know the answer.

8 | Strange to loss

Tedious teacher

12/4   It's 8:00am and I should probably get to work soon.

Last night my mom called to ask, "What should I recommend to my friend with depression?"

Thoughts raced through my head with all the things that could help. There are many alternatives other than drugs, the only option you're usually given.

Her friend had something in her head removed, like a brain tumor or cancer or something. Now she's on the drug Trazadone, probably to help because she can't sleep and is depressed. Her main condition is dystonia, which is a #1 side effect of her medication. It's an endless toxic cycle. They even recommend not giving depressed people

Trazadone because large doses of it can aid in a suicide attempt, stupid!

12/13   Desmond was found murdered in a park. I can't even believe it! We just saw him at Jona's brother's wedding in September. I heard he was heavy into drugs, that was part of the reason he moved back home with his mom and dad. It must have caught up with him, or maybe it was just a fluke, an accident? I'm angry that he's dead. What the f*ck! Why is the one word that keeps repeating in my head. Why did someone have to take his life? People are cruel.

The desperation that overwhelms the masses is just regenerated again and again on TV, replayed for us all to see. Lately we've been watching Planet Earth and Blue Planet DVDs by the BBC, they're intense. I've been discussing with Jona how water acts as a carrier of vibration. When there is a commotion in the water animals sense it.

Mammals and fish are also sensitive to taste (smell) in the water thereby allowing them to find food and survive.

What if air acts as our conductor for vibration? Could we send a message to a loved one just by using our thoughts? I'm not sure telepathy and being psychic accurately describe this, maybe it's the 4th Dimension? I'll have to do more research. All I know is I can think of Jona and he calls me. I can hold a question in my mind for my mom and I swear the phone rings and it's her, ready to offer her answer. These common occurrences happen without conscious thought, what if we all held a conscious thought of benefit and well being? I wonder what would happen if we all invested in a positive, present thought of healing? Who couldn't use a little healing?

12.16   We're leaving tomorrow for Desmond's funeral. I'm still in total disbelief. I've never felt sad like this before. I know it was his karma to exit this world at some time, I just never expected such violence.

I miss you Desmond, you are the coolest. I feel you everywhere I go now, like you're right next to me. I imagine you sitting by me, with that sly look on your face.

He'd say, "Yea they're girl jeans, do they look hot on me or what!?"

They did look hot on him, that was the difference. Desmond wasn't cocky, just super stylie at all times. Even when he had a hang over he'd look beautiful and carry on like no big deal. The girl that was with him is still missing. I hope she's alive and escapes those murderers. They beat Desmond to death and threw him in the water under a bridge. Not my Desmond. How could they not listen to his pleas? What would justify his killing in their minds? I know they will feel their mistake. Although I wish all suffering would end on this planet, I guess everyone has a responsibility to own up to what they have done. The impact of every individual's actions is immense and can be felt everywhere, communal consciousness, remember?

12.26   I wish I could be present. Maybe writing will help me stop crying. I think of Desmond's girlfriend, and wish I could help her in some way relieve the pain. I can't imagine being her, or his parents.

She said, "You're glad you can't imagine."

We hung out with her and her dad on X-mas Eve for a minute and met her two crazy little dogs. It was good to talk about Desmond, look at the thoughtful art he did for her and just hug. I've never felt so much, I can't even describe the thoughts. Useless pointless thoughts, what if I had done this or that? Everything is inevitably linked, I can't separate one part out of the whole to blame for his murder. No one deserves to be murdered, taken without a pause. The world should stop without Desmond, how can it go on? The significance is huge, so large I can't hold it, I have to let it go.

12/29   We were in a white room, then I noticed it was transparent plastic and we were flying above the ground. It was cylinder shaped and lightweight with two ends that opened. All of a sudden Jona fell out the back and I caught him with my fingertips. We were trying to hold on.

WISDOM OF SOFT FUR
DOG

Ode to Rebel

(May 3, 2003 – May 21, 2006)

[re~bel 1:opposing or taking arms against a government or ruler 2:of or relating to rebels 3:disobedient, rebellious.]

Part Two

9 | Thorns protect

Slender and a bit tall with brown eyes and auburn hair I could blend in with most English, Irish and German crowds. Oval face and freckles, fabulous kisses from angels or sun damage dependent upon your life view.

Our apartment is my only sanctuary from the outside world, work, and the threat of a dysfunctional social scene. I live in the mountains with my husband of six months. We are beginning a new year together as newlyweds, it feels like a *dream*.

He has kind blue eyes that calmly take every moment as it arrives, effortlessly. We are the same height and almost exact same weight. Wild golden brown hair he will challenge the wind on a stormy day and come out the victor.

10 | Ego wants escape

Desire flaunts relate

Suffer haunts bait

Jan 8   I'm holding down the fort at work and not doing my reggae show anymore. It just got to be too much, a strain, not something enjoyable like it used to be. It's been dumping mass snow lately, probably 3 feet or more. This morning was a blue bird sky, but now it has turned gray. I must take a toke and get back to work. Jona just called, he's working hard. I'm amazed at how well we get along, even when we fight we always get over it and everything's cool. He's awesome, my total dream man.

1/9   Last night I passed out early. After snowing for 3 days straight it is finally letting up.

1/13   Jona's dad was sick and we went to see him. He was in his bed, not doing well. There were other people there and we were talking to them. I thought to myself I can talk to Jona's dad later, but he was gone later. I felt bad I didn't take the time earlier with him.

1/22   Last night I opened up for Eek A Mouse, it was epic.

The guitar player came up to me and said, "I love the one you just played, Ina Kamoze, Kill Dat Sound Buoy, I haven't heard that since high school."

Another guy in the band said, "I loved your set."

I spun a wicked lineup on the CDJ's, vinyl setting of course. I was definitely nervous and fumbling with the mixer, but once I started it was ok. The band was just arriving and setting up as I played, it was cool they got to hear my whole set. I gave away cds to the keyboardist and guitarist, then went backstage and gave one to Eek A Mouse and his sister. Overall the night was awesome.

1/28   I wish I had something positive to say, but the truth is I want to destroy everything. I feel sad and that sadness turns into anger and frustration too easily. I'm having trouble understanding why I snap and hate the whole world it seems. I love my husband, but have difficulty communicating and I feel like I influence him negatively when I'm upset.

Last week I felt ill and finally got the flu on Friday, my period on Saturday and a head cold on Sunday. Today is Monday --- I fell and skinned my knee, broke the front of my iPhone and cried the rest of the afternoon. It seems funny when I write it down, but I didn't think it was too funny earlier today.

Bummed I was sick and couldn't go out for X-Games, I even missed Jona spinning at a house party. I wish I didn't react to everything so much and would stop getting upset over the past that I can't change. I feel mad about the way I was treated ten years ago, even three years ago. My patience capacity is totally absorbed by these old memories, leaving no tolerance for the moment.

I must release these old messages I constantly say to myself. I don't want to be here needs to be replaced with I want to be here. Instead of saying get away to myself or those around me I need to say stay and help me. I can't take it anymore always pops to mind. The truth is I can take it, infinity. I want to die must be replaced with I want to live. The message I tell myself that I am bad and always say the wrong thing is not true. I am a person who wants to benefit myself and others without judgment of right and wrong. I still need discernment though and thus the battle of mind versus   me continues.

1/30   We were somewhere in a house and there were tons of guards. They didn't want us moving around so we had to sneak around, out of sight. I finally escaped to my house and found the dogs in my old bedroom. I had two girlfriends there and asked, "Why can't you help me?" I felt like I was losing my voice from screaming for help.

1/30   I'm going to see my cranial sacral therapist in a minute and I guess I'm doing alright. If I'm struggling with my practice I must be doing well. Constantly checking my mind, I find a repetitive message of negativity playing. Angry and sad when I've pushed it too long without taking care of myself. I know Jona does everything in his power to help. I simply cannot continue to bring others down when I'm struggling. I know I can continue on a positive path.

I just saw my cranial sacral therapist and it was soothing. We basically talked about how if nothing changes within a belief the same thing will appear in five years, in ten years. Sometimes through experience a belief system can change. For instance, he busted out his credit card and cut it in half.

Meanwhile I protested, "You don't need to do that!"

He asked, "What am I holding?"

I said, "A credit card."

He asked, "What else?"

I said, "It could be an illusion, it could mean power, it could hold some sort of status for some people?"

He then asked, "What does a bush man in Africa think it is?"

I said, "Plastic?"

"Correct, it's dependent upon your concept."

I used to think money was bad and the people that had it were bad, that it only brought pain and suffering. I've worked hard for my money and now that I'm paying my credit card off bit by bit, I know it can bring a lot of relief from suffering. I could get an emergency airlift if needed, I know that money can help. My concept behind money has changed, therefore my belief about it has changed.

1/31   Regarding over-medication and the single sided mindset of the medical community: It is my conclusion that there needs to be an acute care facility to handle individuals that choose an alternative path. The facility would employ every possible modality, all kinds of techniques, be it holistic, or even unexplainable. The person as a whole would be addressed and a gentler approach to wellness would be accessed. Maybe it could be part of a new health care plan that focused on wellness instead of sickness.

11 | Knot bound grip close

Blind hold chips down

Drawn again inhale binge

2/3   My tongue and mouth were swollen and I couldn't breathe. I told Jona, "We have to go to the hospital." I was digging in my drawer for some Benadryl, it was scary.

2/14   This past week we went to see Jona's dad. He had not eaten in 10 days, but was still taking fluids. He was adorable with his beautiful grey faux-hawk hairstyle that had naturally formed since December. We read to him from my book Celestial Gallery and rubbed shea butter on his feet and arms. Although he was out of it, because of the morphine box that shoots out pain relief every 10 minutes, he was still witty and fun.

At one point he said to us, "I've died and gone to heaven."

We all stopped and looked at each other like, what?! It made me realize that death can be warm and light, surrounded by loved ones, released gently into the next world.

After seeing Jona he said, "I am ready to go."

The whole family went into his room and sat with him, giving him love and surrounding him in light.

When Jona and I left him he said, "I'll see you next week."

I remember he was sitting up and Jona and I were hugging him in between us. He put his foot on Jona's foot, it was sweet. There was some part of me that wanted to keep him here, but that was just selfish. I tried with all my might to release my human hold and help him into the current, where he needed to go. It was heartbreaking having to leave him knowing we would never see him again.

2/24   Jona and I were at a huge outdoor concert and we heard a rumor that the government was going to shut it down. We were sitting at a picnic table under an awning when we saw the military come over the hill, no warning, just tear gas and bullets. We ran to find our car, but they were bombing everything and we couldn't get there. We decided to get out and all of a sudden we were at a large wooden house, going down a jagged rock wall to escape. I said, "Let's go the other way." We ran and jumped to the neighboring cliff that was covered with snow. After traversing around a few corners I realized Jona was on the other side and I was incredibly high up on the cliff. We were divided by a river. I thought to myself what if I jump and don't make it?

2/28   It's hard to believe February is almost over. We found out Jona's dad was unresponsive on Wednesday, February 13th, after 24 hours he passed away on February 14th, Valentine's Day. He was an incredible man and I'm proud Jona is his son.

He was surrounded by his family and covered in warm light when he passed. It made me feel differently about death. He made it ok, an inevitability that we all face as soon as we are born. His song that he wrote finally made sense to me, how nothing is ever lost it only changes form. The memorial was calm and peaceful, it brings tears to my eyes to recount. They showed a slideshow of him with his friends and family. There was even a picture of him and I dancing at Jona and my wedding. He had a smile on his face, regardless of his pain. He was always smiling. Always is a strong word, but even on his deathbed when I was rubbing shea butter on his hands and feet he would become conscious for brief moments.

He smiled and said, "Thank you Terra, you are so sweet." That meant the world to me.

Everyone at the memorial had only amazing things to say about him. I feel like I've written this before. Perhaps in a dream, or recently to a friend, I swear I've had these exact thoughts before. He always wanted to know how you were doing, what you were up to. Selfless actions came effortlessly to him. Mentoring people came naturally because everyone looked up to him. He was an honorable man that taught everyone around him to enjoy and live life. Countless people got up and spoke about how they were better people because they knew him. Everyone was proud to have been a part of his life. One guy even broke out into a cappella about him being the Music Man. When all was said and done there was not a dry eye in the house.

It was about his life, not his death. He even had the pleasure of meeting with the minister prior to his memorial to tell him exactly what he wanted him to say. They met over milkshakes and onion rings, no less. The message was clear, love those around you. He didn't want us to be sad, rather, know that everything simply changes form. There was a point when all selfish thoughts of missing him were gone and only joy and tears remained.

He once told Jona, "A man is only as good as his word."

When he asked his father what to think about religion, Gramps told him to, "Eat the steak and leave the bone."

I think that became his philosophy too.

12 | Dry feeling of heat

Wet tears of defeat

No time to retreat

3/7   In a gigantic movie theater with really cushy seats, it reminded me of Vegas. Sitting with all the girls and all of a sudden they moved seats and left me out. I remember Jona going back to hang out with them, hugging all the girls. Then, even though he was my husband, he turned into someone else. My friend was there and wanted to sit with me, she's cool. I said, "Let's go find our rooms." We proceeded to enter a gigantic hotel where we had assigned rooms. Mine opened into a huge loft with beautiful furniture and tons of space. I told her, "I'm going to look for my husband." I knew he was flirting with other girls and I wanted to give my ring back. I wandered the halls until I found them near the elevators. I asked, "Can I stay with

*you guys?" They said, "No," got in the
elevator and left. I felt very sad and left out.
Why had I not stayed and hung out with my
friend?*

3/7   I've written letters to all the previous
places I've been hospitalized, requesting
copies of my medical records. I just received
the first one yesterday from Boulder
Community Hospital at Mapleton. It was good
to read through, it clarified timeframe and
confirmed a few things I already knew. The
cards were stacked against me and the
various assessments are one-sided and
inaccurate in places. It's unclear from their
notes, I'm either 24 or 25 years old upon
arrival from Jamaica and still under the
influence of the major tranquilizer Clopixal.
The staff was unfamiliar with Clopixal so
unfortunately they administered Depakote to
me, a contra indicatory drug to Clopixal. Not a
good idea to mix them. I don't quite

understand how I could be considered manic when all signs show lethargy, slow movements, dazed vision, and pressured speech (lockjaw). I do recall the white room and straightjacket they first put me in, thankfully they didn't tie down the arms. I remember a feeling of wanting to be well, wishing the drugs didn't hurt so much.

There are even notes of the nurses administering Tylenol, which clearly has acetaminophen, A.K.A. speed to me. Overall there is no note regarding when that huge crazy woman attacked me in the family room and tried to strangle me with the phone cord.

They would ask, "How are you, what is your plan?" Ironically even if I had an answer I was still considered sick.

If I didn't know the answer and asked them, "What is the plan," they seemed to think I was getting better.

I felt betrayed by my ex-boyfriend for talking to the doctors about me.

He told them, "She spends money, drives fast and is not taking her medications."

He was my only confidante and now I had no one. The level of anger and frustration was exactly equal to the jumbled mix of drugs they gave me.

Little did the doctor note I had suicide ideation while taking Zoloft. Only now, ten years later, has Pfitzer been taken to court over the risk of suicide for persons under the age of 25 taking Zoloft. At the time the doctors saw no contra indications in taking Depakote with Zoloft. Now the combo has been proven in 2007, to increase mania and rapid cycling. That's what happens when working off a theory or assumption that chemistry can successfully be altered. Other influencing factors are rarely taken into consideration. I believe that my chemistry is exactly as it is meant to be, evolutionary factors   intact.

I wish someone had shown me another path, or some kind of preventative measure that I could have utilized.

3/10   I felt like I had left for the funeral and had not said goodbye to my mom, now I would never see her again. I wished I had hugged her longer, I wish I could see her again. I couldn't, she was gone forever. (I awoke in tears.)

3/11   I was trying to hide, they kept taking people away. I was there with Jona, we had to drive back through Cambodia to catch our plane. I realized our plane was leaving tomorrow and I didn't know what to do. Jona said, "We should sleep in."

3/11   A few days ago I got my medical records from Langley Porter Hospital in San

Francisco. It brought back lots of memories of being confused, misunderstood and judged. I had just gone through a traumatic breakup and didn't have any medical marijuana to keep me balanced. I felt like an innocent trapped in the system. All I wanted to do was expose the shoddy misgivings of the looney bin, but how when no one believes you?

The fear of being trapped and drugged is very real. I know I was sped up and a little out of hand, but the methodologies for normalizing someone are far more traumatic than being sped up. The nurse's observations of me as intrusive, dominating and inappropriate were probably dead on. Yeah, that's just my bad form. It's like having your best friend call you out on all your sh*t, judging your behavior as right or wrong. How can fault be found with my glitter nail polish? Or my tank top for that matter? Didn't they realize I don't own any long sleeved conservative tops?

3/13   I heard a news report yesterday morning that there is a new form of staph infection that is resistant to all antibiotics. They were comparing it to a new A.I.D.S. virus and said it, "Killed 16,000 people last year alone."

I also saw a special on frogs that have mutated to have six legs. They found that a majority of the ponds in Michigan contained these six-legged frogs. When they studied the United States and Canada they found six-legged frogs in 49 states and in parts of Canada. They determined that it could not be a genetic mutation due to the widespread nature, instead the mutation must be caused by the frog's environment. They mentioned the use of pesticides could be to blame.

3/16   My mom called and said, "You're leaving on the plane at 3:10 pm." I was in the house getting ready. We were all in our own blankets, like we'd just gotten up from bed. Jona and I hugged and he felt incredible. I told him, "You feel amazing." There is this warmth between us. Then he was gone and I went outside to find him, but I only found my mom's friends. They reminded me, "You have a plane to catch." I wondered if I was late and went inside to check the time. I went over to the answering machine and there was a message from someone, but I had already missed Jona.

3/26   The real truth is not of concern, only that you know the correct answer. Are you feeling better today? Oh yes, much better. Are you having any side effects from the medication? No, not really. Do you know what your plan is? I'd love if you could help me out with that. Our recommendation is that you follow a regime of taking your medication and continue to seek therapy, either group or individual. Wow, that sounds great, since my medication is working so well I think I'll stick with it this time. How about your drug use when you leave here, do you think you'll continue to drink and smoke? I doubt it, my medication is working well I don't need to self medicate with smoking and drinking. What can you tell me about your stay here? I realize I have a problem that I need to deal with, I'm bipolar and need to take medication to stay balanced. I look forward to therapy and my recovery. Thank you and have a nice day, next patient.

Tell them what they want to hear, don't be too honest, just informative enough for them to make their judgment. Oh, and don't let the revolving money maker hit you on the way out.

Do dreams exhibit judgment? Can you quantify your experience? How many hours make up a lifetime? Are you shortening yours by worrying about living? So many questions.

13 | Hit walls win habits again

Choking gasp desire illusion

Holding grasp quit fire fusion

4/8   We went to visit our friend and his pit bull that was diagnosed with bone cancer in his shoulder about two weeks ago, harsh. His muscle has atrophied and he carries his front right paw like it hurts. I want to help in some way. We just sat on the floor and snuggled up, he loves the attention. He's definitely in pain, which sucks. I love him and wish he would get better, but for whatever reason he's getting worse. The whole death thing is totally unfair. We don't prepare ourselves for the end of the life cycle.

4/21   Work has been great lately. Life is short, I have to live well today and all things will come to me. All my dreams will find me. I've dreamt of being many things, but being a writer was never one of them. Now I feel like my dream is not to be a writer, because I already am one, but to allow others to gain what they may from my experience. I know it is my truth. Love as much as possible, laugh when you don't think you can and everything will be the culmination of your choices.

4/29   Just took my morning toke and lovely clearing of my lungs. Deep thought for the day: there should be an ordinance that all asphalt parking lots be converted to multi-level lots with mandatory trees planted on top.

Today Jona and I are going to open a joint checking account with our tax return, now we can save together, stoked.

Yesterday was hard, lots of tears about change I think. Loss is terrible and my instinct is to make it better, if that isn't defeating. It's like trying to stop the earth from turning, no small illusion. I don't want to think I've given up, but reality sets in. We all look for excuses time, money, blah, blah, blah. I know I can do anything if I set my mind to it.

14 | A friend hung themselves

We ask ourselves why

Lingering in limbo

Trapped in the sky

5/7   Since receiving all of my medical records and combing through them thoroughly I have a different view. I really applaud those Doctor's and nurses for doing the best job they knew how to do. I was definitely not easy to deal with, I remember how hard it was coming from my side, but I never quite knew the impact it had on others. I hope people can forgive me for possibly hurting them unknowingly.

I brought up some of the notes recorded from Mahalona Medical with my psychotherapist.

I honestly think I was hallucinating from drug toxicity, the walls and floors were moving.

She said, "It's normal for a person with psychosis to pick at the floor or pick at the walls."

Couldn't it have been from the heavy drugs they had me on? Maybe it is common, I don't know. I'm going to attempt to decipher the hospital notes to give another perspective, I'm documented alright.

It makes me not want to publish my book, I get scared of what people will think. Then, I remember if I had died in that hospital no book would ever be written. I feel like I died in that cold white room with crawling walls. My fight gave way to hunger and thirst, or maybe I came to when they reduced my meds. Either way 13 days refusing food and water did nothing for my looks. Besides the obvious weight loss, refusing all help means my teeth became gross and dirty from not brushing, my hair became tangled and knotted, my skin became rashy and irritated from not showering and the retribution on my nutrient stores was brutal. Fatty acids, anyone?

I guess it was my choice, or a gigantic string of choices as my journal illustrates. I am currently not on any medication and have not been since July three years ago. I'm fine with the occasional migraine or leg cramps, it's way better than the potential side effects from the drugs. True, I've been known to fall asleep at 9:00pm, but it could be as early as 6:00pm, or whenever I'm tired. I've also been known to stay up all night, or wake in the middle of the night and stay up. Sometimes I'm not hungry and other times I eat a bunch.

Basically the philosophy is it's ok to cry, eat when hungry, sleep when tired. Other than that, what you put in your body is up to you. Even I can't control my love of pastries at times.

I'm bummed, our friend had to put his beautiful pit bull down, his bone cancer was knarly and he was in tons of pain. It must be terrible to lose your best friend of 12 years. He was such a loyal, outstanding dog. We will greatly miss his howling-growl-talk that he addressed us with, and that friendly whip of a tail that made you realize his power. I'll miss him, I don't want to let him go. I can't believe he's gone, he brought joy to everyone he met. I will keep a special spot for him in my heart, remembering his cutie eyes and soft fur that would itch you later. He was always up for playing and cuddling. We'll all miss him desperately.

15 | Couldn't take it
Had to flee running
Wouldn't make it
Judgmentally

June 3   We just got back from Vegas, it was awesome. We stayed at New York, New York and rode the roller coaster a bunch. I totally have bruises on my elbow and shoulder from too much 'coastering. I loved the attraction Dolphin Habitat at the Mirage, I was blown away at the dolphin's presence, just awe-striking! At the last tank we saw one of the female dolphins jump out of the water and slide up on the smooth bank next to Jona and me. She showed off her beautiful physique and her baby dolphin slid up, snuggled for a second, then splash back in the water. The mama was still posing beautifully, her blue skin shimmering and glowing with camouflage stripes. It was absolutely incredible, my own dolphin experience. Only Jona and I were at the tank's edge, the trainers had already gone, so I know the dolphins were showing us love. I feel blessed to have spoken with a dolphin, it was life changing.

Then we saw the lions, white and Bengal-striped tigers, a snow leopard, cheetahs, and some funky llama-camel guys. We went to the wax museum, which was interesting and fun, but no comparison to the dolphins. The next day we ate at Paris for my birthday and went to Mandalay Bay to the Shark Walk. It was intense seeing all of that marine life up close and personal. Overall the trip was a blast.

I definitely had my hormonal moments topped with a little insecurity and self-torture, but who doesn't? Things pass and my catatonic state of fleeing my body ends in a re-emergence with a new experience and a grounding kiss from my sweetie. We all evolve and change. No one promised it would turn out the first time we tried to balance ourselves. Try, try again, until success is eminent. I'm going to cry again and I'm going to laugh again, hopefully intertwined. Acceptance of oneself is not always easy, but it is necessary.

16 | Let's all just be

Sorrow left behind

Given to sit on our minds

Unanswered cries selfish lies

8/9   July flew by, I'm not quite sure what happened.

8/10   Mom went to a conference last week and found a new therapy for bipolar called Brain Spotting. It sounds a lot like Cranial Sacral Therapy which is based on the fact that the plates in the human skull move. It makes sense that relieving the pressure on whatever part of the brain that is adversely affected would relieve the symptoms of the pressure.

I think mental illness is relating to trauma in a helpless state. Instead of being empowered to heal oneself we focus on the sickness and what is wrong. What about what is right? Where are the shamans to guide us into the new world we've created? Come forward and realize that you are what you've always been and will always be, full of infinite potential.

8/23 I've learned so much about my path sorting through my journals. I just realized they used Inapsine on me in Hawaii. Not the recommended 2.5mg, but 10mg to my right and left legs. It explains a lot, the muscle rigidity and inability to talk. The combination of Inapsine with a CNS (central nervous system) depressant such as Depakote is contraindicative. I'm glad it didn't kill me.

I was talking with my mom about it and she said, "You were hallucinating before you went into the hospital."

Oh really, and how would you know that? Channeling is very different from seeing bugs crawling on the walls.

My mom confirmed it though, "I could tell it wasn't you, the voice sounded different."

I knew I was not myself. I was Mana. Which was odd since, at the time, I had not previously known that name. While recently researching it's meaning I remembered I had split a mushroom chocolate before I became manna. It makes more sense now.

17 | Told to oneself

Trying to hide

Choices revealed

Finally healed

9/2   It's yours, you made it, you created it, own it. My friend is cool, he gave me three Patron Passes and three backstage passes to see Widespread Panic. I took a few friends and we had a blast. I haven't danced in a long time. Sometimes I think all Widespread sounds the same, but then they'll bust into one I know and it's like an old love affair. I'm singing along with JB and doing my liberating hippy dance. Although I was tired and went home by 9:15pm, I'm proud I was social and didn't let my insecurities keep me at home. I want to see people, I want to hang out and have fun. I can do it.

I think of JB singing, "Can't get high, can't get it right."

It's like, without you, there is nothing, "Drag my whole body under..."

9/12   It's rainy out today, hurricane Ike is nailing the Texas and Louisiana coastline.

9/6   *I dreamt I was painting in black. I covered up the ray of yellow coming from the bottom of the canvas. I thought maybe I can paint a ray of light there later.*

9/8   *I was going somewhere and Mom dropped me off. She had left and was waiting in line. I ran up to her and said, "I don't want to leave you!" There was a tear coming down her cheek and we hugged.*

9/16   I was at a huge house on the top of a hill at a party. I remember looking in the mirror and seeing myself and Jona with a baby. Could it be our baby? I went to the door and it was snowing outside. Then all of a sudden someone pushed this girl next to me down the stairs, then they pushed me down the stairs. There was so much snow I just kept falling and falling, down the hill. Then two other girls and I huddled together in the pitch black and tried to find our way back. All these shadowy animal figures kept running by us. It could have been a buffalo, or maybe a bear. It was hard to see, all we could do was stop and stay close to the ground.

9/17   We were watching the dogs and there was a black puppy. We left and when we came back we couldn't find it. I ran downstairs to check, but I forgot the key. When I came back up I saw the puppy hanging from the wall. It looked like it was attached to a cord or wire. I screamed so loud nothing came out. I ran to get Jona. He lifted the puppy down and it was fine. The electric current was holding it against the wall before Jona saved it.

10/5   I went to the doctor to see what was going on with my hip. They did some tests and came back with an x-ray of these sperms swimming up my canal. They told me I was pregnant.

DREAMING REALITY

Now four years later, my son is a year old and the light of our lives. We are blessed he has come to renew our knowledge of love and compassion.

The unseen dimension within each of us grants us the ability to heal ourselves and access a higher knowing. My deepest wish is that we will all focus on healing our own hearts, for only then will we be able to heal humanity.

The end.

ABOUT THE AUTHOR

Focusing on art, journaling and poetry,
Trevi Bennett has had the opportunity to
process and assimilate her work into an
observation of the experiment life. After
studying abroad in Europe, she graduated with
a Bachelors in Fine Art from the University of
Colorado, Boulder, and has shown her water-
based oil paintings in California and Colorado.
She can be found creating, listening to music,
playing, writing, skiing and hiking.

www.ingramcontent.com/pod-product-compliance
Lightning Source LLC
Chambersburg PA
CBHW070548030426
42337CB00016B/2411